Gratitude

Discover How To Gain Emotional Freedom Through The Power Of Gratitude

By Ace McCloud
Copyright © 2015

Disclaimer

The information provided in this book is designed to provide helpful information on the subjects discussed. This book is not meant to be used, nor should it be used, to diagnose or treat any medical condition. For diagnosis or treatment of any medical problem, consult your own physician. The publisher and author are not responsible for any specific health or allergy needs that may require medical supervision and are not liable for any damages or negative consequences from any treatment, action, application or preparation, to any person reading or following the information in this book. Any references included are provided for informational purposes only. Readers should be aware that any websites or links listed in this book may change.

Table of Contents

Introduction 6
Chapter 1 – Why is Getting Grateful so Powerful? 9
Chapter 2 – What Benefits Can I Expect From Getting Grateful? 13
Chapter 3 – What is Gratefulness Practice and How Do I Start? 18
Chapter 4 – Ten Simple Ways to Get Grateful 20
Chapter 5 – Want a little extra Happiness? 26
Chapter 6 – How to Make Gratitude a Habit 29
Conclusion 32
My Other Books and Audio Books 33

Be sure to check out my website for all my Books and Audio books.

www.AcesEbooks.com

Introduction

I want to thank you and congratulate you for buying the book, "Gratitude: Discover How To Gain Emotional Freedom Through The Power Of Gratitude."

So your life isn't that great? You see everyone around you and they are happier, healthier, achieving more and doing more than you think you ever think you could? I am going to let you know a little secret - more often than not they don't actually have any more of anything than you do. What they do have however, is a sense of gratitude for what they ALREADY have in their lives – so rather than bemoaning what they lack, they are busy getting on with life as it happens and enjoying things while they have them, rather than constantly waiting for the next big thing to arrive.

When did you last look at your car and get thankful for its presence in your life? I bet you are far more likely to be dreaming about the one you intend to replace it with, or are busy moaning about how much it costs each year to run it and keep it in good condition. How about your spouse or partner – when did you last look at them and honestly say thank you for all the incredible things they do for you, rather than getting unhappy about all the things they don't do right? It is a simple thing – but what you appreciate, appreciates! If you aren't grateful for what is already there, why would anything or anyone new feel drawn to you and want to stick around?

This book contains proven steps and strategies on how to make gratefulness a part of your daily life. Gratefulness can transform your emotional and physical health along with a variety of other beneficial aspects in your life. I will show you scientifically proven methods that are simple to do, and so easy to implement into your daily life that you may even question whether they can possibly work – but they do – and have been proven to do so by some of the best university research teams in the world.

I have been working in the arena of peak performance, therapy and wellbeing for many years. I have been privileged to work with many clients as they transform their lives for the better, and have written a lot of books on how you can get the most out of your life. I have spent months researching this subject to ensure you get the most up to date and excitingly straightforward advice I can get to you. I can categorically say that the largest positive changes in people's lives that I have seen have come about once they have started to make gratitude a part of their daily wellbeing practice.

Absolutely everyone can benefit from the techniques in this book. How many of us are really grateful for the life we have, the health we enjoy, or the things we own? And even if we are, how often do we actually make a point of stating out loud and proud that gratitude? Yet many of us are also suffering with depression, anxiety, stress and the constant drive to have more, do more and be more – it is never-ending, and it is no wonder that some feel that depressed about this. I want the information in this book to help you to put that feeling of lack away out of sight for good. Let's get you feeling abundant, that your life is already full of promise, great people and things – without you spending another penny to make it happen!

As I was researching this book, I decided to implement a new daily gratitude practice and I can honestly say that even I have been amazed at how much of an impact it has had on my mood and wellbeing. I like to think I am a pretty positive and pro-active person, but I definitely have more energy, more drive and a lot more belief in myself that I really can do whatever is on my to-do list each day now. A client of mine started a gratitude practice, she suffers from ME/CFS, and within days she noticed an improvement in her energy levels, and now just a few months on she is preparing to return to work full time as she feels like her old self again – despite her doctors telling her that recovery would be long and it would be unlikely that she would be able to ever return to full time work. Though we have implemented a number of different techniques, we started with gratitude, and she credits this as being the number one tool that has impacted her recovery – without it she wouldn't have felt well enough to even consider trying any of the others.

If you follow through on even one of the tips and techniques I will tell you about in this book, then I guarantee you that you will see a massive step change in how great your life, health and wealth are within months. If you make them a part of your life forever, I promise you that you will be happier, healthier and have more energy if you just stay consistent. You too can achieve the benefits to your wellbeing, and begin to enjoy a sense of peace and joy in your life as it is right now – with nothing else added that I and many others have seen when they implement the Power of Gratitude. It's easy – you just have to get in the habit of getting grateful on a daily basis!

Don't hang around constantly waiting for that lottery win, or that fantastic new job that you believe will change everything to come along to change your life. Don't wait until you have lost 10 pounds to go on that beach holiday, or activity filled trip. Do it now! Your body and mind have everything they already need for you to be able to live a fantastic life – if you are prepared to spend just a few moments a day acknowledging how wonderful your life already is – and if you focus on the good stuff, you will get more good stuff! Because the simple truth in life is that you get what you focus on, and if that is all the stuff your life lacks then it isn't going to be pretty (and that lottery win or awesome job simply isn't going to ever materialize). Get grateful for what you do have now. Live in the present, not the past or the future, and get the life you want now without spending a dollar more than you paid for this book!

The techniques in this book have been proven time and again, in real life and in research labs around the world to truly have an impact on the quality of people's lives. From Oprah, to Tony Robbins, Bruce Lee and many others, all of us who get grateful will testify with our hand on our hearts, that this simple, and cost free habit has changed our lives. I know I will never stop being grateful for everything I am blessed to be and have now, and I know that by doing so I can change my mood and energy levels in a moment – and even better, attract even more to be grateful for into my life! Don't you want that too? If you do, then just keep on reading – the answers are all inside.

Chapter 1 – Why is Getting Grateful so Powerful?

Gratitude, it is such a simple thing, so why aren't we all doing it? I am sure your Mom and Dad encouraged you as a kid to say thank you when you were given gifts or compliments, even when Aunt Mabel didn't quite keep up with the trends in modern life and gave us a gift right out of the Ark. I am sure that for most of you that they taught you to give thanks not just at Thanksgiving, but before every meal, and at every prayer time as you went to bed. They encouraged us by giving us praise when we got things right, and so wanting to earn more of that praise we often did more things to make them happy; and unwittingly learned that when we want somebody to do something for us the best way is not to castigate them, but to foster a sense of mutual benefit and gratitude. Yet somewhere between being a small child, full of wonder and delight with the world and becoming a teenager we seem to lose this fantastic habit of being grateful. We start to receive less praise for our efforts, and so we become less co-operative with others, we give less praise and support to our friends and families and begin to believe that we aren't loved as much because otherwise we wouldn't have to be the one that is always doing things for everyone else and never receiving anything in return.

But I want you to stop and think right now:

- When was the last time you sat down at the dinner table to say grace and thank God/the Universe or even your job for the ability to provide this meal?

- When did you last say thank you for your health, your home, or your car?

- When did you encourage someone to do something for you, rather than demand it?

- When was the last time you genuinely thanked them for doing as you asked?

- When was the last time you received praise and thanks from your boss for having done a good job?

- When did you last take not of all the wonderful things you already have in your life?

- When was the last time you told a friend just why they mean so much to you?

- When did you last say thank you, and genuinely mean it from the bottom of your heart?

Most of us lose our childlike sense of wonder at the world right around the time we stop being grateful for everything that comes into our lives. We blame it on being busy, or that we just don't have what we wanted – that life hasn't turned out the way we planned. But a small child is often just as thrilled by the packaging of a gift as they are with the gift itself, and that gratitude fuels their imagination to create wonderful games, and incredible box-built structures. They don't often mind that what is in the box wasn't exactly what was on their list – they are grateful that anything at all was, and will proceed to create new games, and create wonderful new worlds in which to enjoy the new toy and its box. As an adult, it is rare that we even wrap a gift properly for one another – let alone be transported by the effort someone has put in to make something so simple look so wonderful for us. We take it for granted that people will know our taste, and are disappointed when we realize they don't know us as well as we thought when the gift isn't something we wanted. We say thank you grudgingly as we know we should be polite, but are already planning where we can hide it so they don't know how much we don't like it. Rather than being grateful for a friend or loved one who cares enough about us to buy us a gift at all, which is an incredible blessing in and of itself, whatever they may buy us, we are selfishly only thinking about our own ego's want list and the fact that this just wasn't on it. We blame our lack of a great job; the wrong house or car; our inability to afford the nicest clothes and all manner of materialistic wants get in the way of appreciating the life we already have.

Research at many major universities is beginning to show us that not only does being grateful give benefits of positive self esteem, and connection to the person who we say thank you to, but that just by being grateful we can improve our own health and wellbeing too. From brain scans to psychological testing, the results are showing massive improvements in people's cognitive, physical, emotional, and spiritual wellbeing from following a program of simple daily gratitude. Sadly, it would appear that we don't come hard-wired to be grateful, and like so many truly useful life skills – like talking, walking and being able to fend for ourselves, it is one we need to work at. Dr Emmons says there are three stages to this in his book "Thanks! How practicing gratitude can make you happier." These are: recognizing what we are grateful for; acknowledging our gratitude; and actually appreciating it. Simple right?

In an 8 year long study, Emmons has shown conclusively that regular gratitude practice results in:

- Improvements in progress towards personal goals
- Higher alertness
- Greater enthusiasm
- Becoming more determined
- More attention to detail
- Greater energy levels

- Better health markers
- Improved sleep quality and duration
- Greater levels of optimism
- Increased positive mood
- Greater sense of connection and feelings for others

I really hope that this has started to get your attention as to why this simple tool is so powerful - this is a pretty impressive list, and the results showed that the moment you shift your mindset from a negative one to one of appreciation that brain function becomes better balanced, harmonized and supple; the heart begins to pump in a more coherent and rhythmic manner; and that biochemical changes trigger healthful responses throughout the body. People pay thousands in medical insurance to get some of these benefits, and they can be achieved by doing a simple five minute gratitude practice daily. I don't know about you – but I think I will go for the 5 minutes a day!

A further study is currently being undertaken at the Greater Good Science Centre at UC Berkely, and it will be incredibly exciting to see what it will add to the already blooming picture that research into gratitude is giving us. Psychiatric and Psychology departments in Universities all over the world are proving over and over again just how much of an impact the simple things in life make to our health – and though it often takes a while for this stuff to be disseminated, the information is out there, and you can start to get the most from it right now.

I found this fantastic YouTube video called "The Science of Happiness" by SoulPancake during my research, and I love the straightforward way that it shows the incredible transformative power of the simple act of telling someone how grateful you are for them and the reasons why. Quite simply, this simple act can bring on a whole range of emotions, can make you feel truly connected in a way you probably haven't felt in a while and the bonus is that it makes the other person feel great as well. In this small study, the people at The Science of Happiness asked people to undertake a happiness questionnaire, and then asked them to write a letter to someone they felt was incredible, amazing or who had made a massive impact on their life. They were then asked to call them. A happiness questionnaire was then again filled out with the questions randomized so that participants were unaware it was the same test they took earlier.

The results were quite incredible, and I will admit I really didn't think that such a simple exercise, done just once, could possibly have a massive effect on anyone. But, I was completely wrong! For all those who wrote down something about the person they were thinking of each of them showed an increase in happiness of between 2 and 4%. Small fry I guess, but still pretty impressive for just writing a few nice things down about someone. For those who called the person, there was a change in happiness score of 4-19%, which I think you will agree is pretty substantial. The most interesting thing about this study was that the person with the lowest score to start with (in other words the unhappiest person) showed the biggest change in their happiness score following this exercise!

The studies all show the same thing, that happiness is improved by being grateful – and that those who are the most unhappy will see the biggest change in their happiness, and the simple truth is that if you change yourself, you will change the world. Just imagine a world where everyone was grateful, where everything was run on the principles of increasing gross national happiness – rather than gross national profit? Can't imagine it? Then take a visit to Bhutan if you can, where exactly that principle is employed in the running of the country. As I am sure you can imagine, it is a calm, peaceful and pleasant place to be a citizen. We may not be able to change the way our governments run the country we live in to one where citizens health and happiness is the key motivator - well maybe not yet anyway – but we can make small changes in our own lives that will lead to massive improvements for us personally.

As Jane Ransom says in her YouTube Video called "Discover The Three Keys To Gratitude" by TedX Talks, great teachers don't need the biggest IQ's, they need the biggest hearts. It is people with big hearts who practice gratitude, and it is people with big hearts who bit by bit change the world around them into a more harmonious and peaceful place to inhabit. It improves self confidence, increases self-discipline and makes us better able to achieve our goals – and makes us a pleasure to be around. That kid at school who no matter how much they were bullied for being different, still managed to be kind and supportive to others – even their tormentors; the guy at work who always has a kind word to say about everyone, even as they go past him on the promotional ladder; the therapist who opens her heart and her life to make everyone feel valued and special, yet whose clients disappear as soon as they are fixed without so much as a thank you; the child in Africa whose one dream is to go to school, whose home is a shack, yet smiles because life is a gift and there is so much to be hopeful for. The difference between us all is quite simply is the amount of gratitude we express. Simple huh?

These are the people in the world that we all secretly long to have the courage to be like – yet we allow our fear and our sense of lack take charge and overwhelm us, in order to keep up with the Jones's. In many cases, these people have so much less than us – yet their gratitude for what they do have is so much greater than ours. This is how they can be at peace and even happy in situations that to us seem insurmountable and unbearable. So, get grateful now that you picked up this book, as it is going to teach you the easiest way to improving all the key aspects of your life. I just want to let you know that I am grateful you have stuck with me this far, I hope you are grateful you have too.

Chapter 2 – What Benefits Can I Expect From Getting Grateful?

Well, I have already given a brief outline of these in Chapter one, but there are at least 31, according to Amit Amin who conducted an incredible meta-analysis of over 26 studies on gratitude that you can see here: http://happierhuman.com/the-science-of-gratitude/. The science is pretty compelling when you look at it, and includes research from some of the top names in psychology and psychiatry. This is only a short book, so I won't go into all 31 of the benefits that Amit suggests – mainly because I feel a lot of them overlap one another. But, put simply, this is your Top Six reasons why you need to read Chapter 3 and get practicing today!

The Top Six Reasons to Get Grateful

1. Quite simply, gratitude *makes us happier*. When you give a compliment, or receive a gift and are truly thankful for it, you will instantly improve your mood. Just think about the last time you received a gift that you truly wanted. It was my fortieth birthday recently, and I received a number of gifts and was truly grateful for every single one of them. However, there were two gifts in particular that completely changed my day and made me get all warm and fuzzy inside. The first was a gift from my brother and sister-in-law. I will be honest, neither of them has been that great at gifts in the past – they tend to buy us what they would like to receive or think is useful, rather than really thinking about the likes and dislikes of who they are buying for. But wow, they clearly thought about it this time. I love music, and theatre and going to festivals – and they generously gifted me with a voucher so I can buy tickets for me and my friends to go and see pretty much whatever we want. I cannot tell you just how happy this made me, and I couldn't wait to call both of them and gush with gratitude for such a truly thoughtful gift. The second was from a very good friend. Again she had thought carefully about the things I enjoy, and had bought me a voucher to spend an afternoon making pots and painting them. This is a gift that is so very much what I love to do and the attention to detail on the gift was truly treasured. But, not only did I get massive pleasure from receiving these gifts, and was over the moon with my gratitude, but the response I got from them when I called to say thank you showed me quite clearly that my gratitude was equally as beneficial for them too.

   The research shows that a five minute gratitude journaling exercise can increase your long term wellbeing by over 10% - the same amount as doubling your income does! Gratitude however, unlike money, is the gift that keeps on giving. The problem with an increasing income is that we tend to spend more, and unless we are truly grateful for the new things we are spending it on, the increase in our health and happiness is short-term. Gratefulness, however, improves our emotions, health, relationships, personality and career – and the effects of daily practice are cumulative – rather than decreasing in gratitude, we find we have so much more to be grateful for!

2. Gratitude *makes us more popular*. This is pretty self explanatory – when you are approved of and told so in a genuine and heartfelt way how does that make you feel? Pretty good right? You probably want to spend more time with that person who approves of you and has such a high opinion of you that they are prepared to tell you so, and you will find yourself wanting to please them even further in most cases. Well, think about if you went around showing others exactly how you feel about them on a regular basis, maybe that feeling of loneliness that you currently may be experiencing may just fade away, as people will want to be around you more when they know their presence is valued and appreciated.

The studies showed that gratitude increases our social capital (those who were just 10% more grateful had 17.5% more social capital) – by that I mean people perceive grateful people to be more trustworthy, nicer, more sociable and appreciative. This has a fantastic added effect of improving the quality of our friendships, working relationships and our marriages. We make deeper connections with people, increasing our amount of friends, and they are healthier more balanced relationships too. Also, as if all that wasn't enough, people who are more grateful are perceived to be kinder and more loving. So like your Mom taught you – remember your pleases and thank yous!

3. Gratitude *improves our personality*. People who regularly practice gratitude were found to be less materialistic; less self-centered; more optimistic; with increased self esteem; and were also more spiritual. These are really important things in our ever more anxiety driven society. We all feel under pressure to keep up with the herd, but grateful people seem to feel this is less of a need for them. Why not take a little pressure off yourself, getting grateful is the best way to learn how to like yourself the way you actually are – rather than waiting until you become magically better when you get that new job, or get in perfect shape!

Just by being more grateful one of my clients found that his social life suddenly improved, within just a few weeks of starting his gratitude practice he went from being the one left out of the invites to company events to being amongst the first to be included. Quite simply he was suddenly more visible, and because he was so positive, and seemed so kind everyone wanted to be around him more. He hadn't actually changed, but he had gotten better at letting people know how he felt when someone helped him to use the copier, or brought him a coffee. Simple things truly can have massive impacts on your life.

4. Gratitude can *improve our career prospects*. The more gratitude you possess, the greater your management skills will be; you will be better at networking and building relationships with your colleagues; you will find that achieving your goals is far easier; you will be confident to make decisions; and you will be more productive. Consider the fact that over 65% of American received no recognition in the workplace last year, and you can understand why so many people are disenchanted with their working lives. If management implemented an 'attitude of gratitude' how much more effective might those workplaces become?

Just think about the last time you worked for someone who truly appreciated the work you did for them? I sincerely hope there is at least one manager in your past that did. Think back to how much more pleasant the working environment was under this supportive boss. Think about the benefits to your wellbeing this positive feedback had, and the effect it had on your work? Now think about a manager who rarely gives compliments, and the effect that has on your wellbeing and work output.

We have all had good and bad managers over the years, but it is incredible how much of an impact they can have on us. One of my clients was telling me just the other day that she had loved her job until about 18 months ago when a new management team was brought in. She felt that this new team expected considerably more from staff, but gave nothing in return, not even by way of verbally acknowledging the team's efforts in trying to deliver it. She was highly dismayed by the change in the atmosphere in the office, and the morale of the team. It is sad but true that a bad boss can make a great job a terrible one, but a truly encouraging thought that a good boss who shows their gratitude for your input can make a terrible job seem fantastic. This is one of the main reasons I decided to become an author. I could control my own work environment without worrying about all the distractions and negativity in a typical work place.

5. Gratitude *improves our emotional wellbeing*. Gratitude makes us more positive; more relaxed and more resilient to life's knocks. Those who practice gratitude also showed a marked difference in the amount of positive memories they can recall, and they are generally less envious of others. What a way to live your life right?

Just think about the last time you received a heartfelt compliment. Were you able to feel mean towards the person who gave you that compliment (even if they had done something dreadful and you had been dreading spending time with them right up until that point)? If someone has just told you how much they love you did a comment from someone less important that may not be as supportive have any impact on you at all? One of the most obvious times that we see the effect of this is when we begin a new relationship. In our hazy glow it feels like nothing can touch us, complaints and insults simply bounce off our invisible shield wall – yet we feel all warm and fuzzy with every new positive thing we experience. This is what gratitude and feeling appreciated does for us.

6. Finally, *gratitude improves our health.* If you decided to practice gratitude for no other reason it should be for this one. The studies show that daily gratitude practice leads to improved sleep; less days off sick and fewer visits to the doctor than those who don't practice gratitude daily; they had longer life spans; increased energy; and they were motivated to eat better and take more exercise.

I have always struggled with sleep, and a few other complaints and it was for this reason that I began a gratitude practice years ago. Once I got my sleep under control though, I made the foolish mistake of letting my gratitude practice go, and not surprisingly some of the other symptoms of headaches; digestive troubles; anxiety; not taking proper care of myself all came back too. Now I am back on a three times a day gratitude prescription I find that all of these things are starting to sort themselves out again – and for something so simple to have such a big effect, I know I am truly grateful! A great thing to do is to go on a walk outside and while you are doing this just think about all the many things you can be grateful for. If you are truly good at it, you should be able to think of hundreds of things.

One of the most interesting studies undertaken on this subject was done by the Gottman Institute. They were able to postulate a ratio which could predict with 90% accuracy whether a marriage would last after an observation period of just three minutes of interactions. They suggested that this gratitude ratio was the number one indicator they had found to predict marital success. The ratio is 5:1. Five positive statements to one negative one. Their findings suggested that if you want to have a successful marriage, you had better make sure that your ratio is no lower than that, and if you want to turn a troubled relationship around, then try to make sure you say at least five positive things to your partner for every one that isn't so supportive!

Prasanna Ranganathan talked about how gratitude changed his life in a moving article on The Huffington Post. He started using a gratitude journal following on from the inspiration and advice of Oprah Winfrey, who in her shows and programs extols its virtues as being the biggest part of her success practice. He started by just jotting down a few things before bed, and said that he found it quite difficult at first because he was so used to thinking about all of the bad things, wallowing in what he then felt was justifiable annoyance at the things that were all going wrong for him. Early entries were apparently along the lines of being grateful that the worst case scenarios he had been envisioning did not occur! But, in time he began to spot what he calls "the small pockets of light and love" in his life. I will tell you about one of his methods he now uses later in this book, but he says that by undertaking this practice he has learned to live far more in the moment, and to truly value the world around him far more.

So, put simply, gratitude for what you have will dramatically change the quality of your life in all the key areas that most of us complain are not working out so well. I can't think of any reason why you would not want to get hot-footing off to the next chapter to find out how.

Chapter 3 – What is Gratefulness Practice and How Do I Start?

Gratefulness Practice is exactly what it says. It is a daily undertaking to make time to get grateful! Because you may be a little rusty on the skills needed, you will need to make a daily effort to practice the new skill until it becomes second nature. You want this to be as much a habit as getting up, as walking, as breathing. It is in many ways just as vital to our effective functioning as those key tasks of breathing, sleeping, eating and drinking – yet so often, just like those four keys to a healthy body, mind, and spirit get neglected in favor of over things!

Jane Ransom in her YouTube video says that the three keys to gratitude practice are:

1. EMOTE – you need to really feel the emotion of gratitude when you undertake your practice – don't just mindlessly say 'I am thankful for…..' You need to really and truly mean it. Take a moment to really think about what you are grateful for in that moment.

2. EXTEND – you need to include others – don't just keep your love and gratitude for friends and family, colleagues or pets inside yourself. You have to tell them – let them know just how grateful you are. Maybe even choose one of the social media sites, or online gratitude apps and websites to post your gratitude and share it with the entire world.

3. And EXERCISE – you need to do it daily, to train those gratitude muscles! As I have already mentioned, gratitude is a skill that we need to learn, and that means practice. Just like learning to walk, or riding a bike, you need to train your mental muscles to make this a habit, so it is as natural a part of your day as walking to your car – you shouldn't need to consciously think about doing this, but for a while you will do – just like any new skill.

So, now that you know the key factors to gratitude practice, you can start pretty simply – just start with a gratitude journal and just make a note of a few things every day that you are grateful for. Do this first thing in the morning, and last thing at night. By undertaking your practice as your day starts, and as it ends you will be ensuring that you start your day in a positive way, and end it feeling optimistic for the adventures ahead.

Oprah believes that there is 'Power in the Words' - that by writing down at least three to five things a day that you are truly grateful for you will, just by this simple and conscious act, make them more concrete. You can hear her talk about gratefulness and her daily journaling practice by checking out her YouTube Video called "Oprah's Gratitude Journal" by OWN TV. She firmly believes that if you focus on what you already have, you will get more to focus on – but if you focus on what you don't have, that you will never have enough – and that is very true.

Again (key point – needs repeating!) we get what we focus on, so it is time to start focusing on how many amazing things you already have in your life.

I started my gratitude practice a number of years ago, and I noticed lots of changes, but foolishly like so many people once I started to feel the benefits I started to let the discipline slip. Not surprisingly I started to notice the little dips in my health; the lack of desire to feed my body healthful foods; the utter inability to drag my butt off the couch to go for a walk; my business started to flag – and worst of all I started to lose the spark that keeps me motivated to write. I caught myself, and decided that maybe by writing a book on the power of gratitude I could kick start myself into beginning a new gratitude practice. I am so glad that I took that decision, and am so grateful to this process, because by undertaking the research for this book I have been able to remember all the changes that this simple tool brought to my life in the past and how much more may happen if I started it up again, and stuck to it this time.

I chose to undertake my challenge quite publicly – I began to post three times a day on Facebook and Twitter and I posted just three things that I am grateful for in that moment. My commitment to this was for one month, and then I reverted back to just using my journal. Even in the thirty days of posting publicly, I began to look forward to waking up in the morning, and doing my gratitude practice as my days really were starting in a much more positive way. I topped myself up at lunchtime – usually after taking a short walk to clear my head and let ideas for my books percolate. And my final post was at night time, just before I went to bed so I could look back at the good things in my day rather than dwelling on the bad ones. I found that I was making better food choices without even thinking about it. I looked forward to my walks rather than them being a chore – I am always so excited to see the new changes in nature each day. Having continued my gratitude practice past that original thirty days, I am also finding it easier to stick to my chosen word count or research requirements each day – and most days I am actually exceeding them, but in less time. I am busy and productive, and I feel so much more positive. I have my dips in the day – but I just quickly think of a few things to be grateful for and find I am right back on track.

Chapter 4 – Ten Simple Ways to Get Grateful

I am sure you can agree that the benefits of being grateful are pretty impressive, and all of them are results that all of us claim to want to implement into our lives – yet for some reason you have that little nagging doubt at the back of your mind that this is just not scientific enough, or can't possibly work for you. You aren't alone. When it comes down to it, most people simply don't ever get around to implementing this super simple technique into their lives with sufficient regularity to let it have an impact. So why don't we do it?

Well, there are a few reasons and the first is that it probably does just sound too easy. Gratitude is deceptively simple, and if it really were that easy surely everyone would be doing it and our doctors would be recommending that rather than pumping us full of painkillers, anti-depressants, blood pressure meds, and statins right? Well, there has been research evidence that gratitude practice, meditation and mindfulness can all reduce pain, increase longevity, and are more effective than drugs for mild to moderate anxiety and depression. It definitely seems like more people need to get involved into integrating this into the world!

Then there is the fear of putting ourselves out there, getting vulnerable or being that little bit different. I have to say I think that this is one of the best things about being a grateful person – I get to bring joy to other people every day, just by being appreciative of their effort and telling them so. I can tell someone that I really like their hair, that their sweater made me smile, or that I simply grateful to have someone to say hello to. I have not once been rebuffed in my positive approach – in fact I get to see faces light up with joy that someone has noticed them and the effort they put in to being good at their job, or looking great, or simply being alive.

Or are you guilty of assuming that others already know how grateful you are for them being in your life? We humans as a race have a terrible tendency of taking so much for granted from the water we drink, to the food on our table, to the presence of our spouse and friends. It is good to know that we are wanted – and therefore if you want to hear it from others, you need to tell them it first! What we give out we will get back!

The final reason we often don't bother with gratitude practice is because the prevailing views in our society are those of greed, competition and selfishness. It is deemed perfectly okay to trample over anyone in your quest for the top – however, try and remember the old adage "Be careful who you tread on as you work your way up, you may just need their help when you are on your way back down!" Be kind, support others and they will support you. We are stronger together, and rather than suppressing someone else's talent, we should be showcasing it. If they do well and we have encouraged and supported them, they are likely to take us with them on their journey – and your kindness and support may just help them to continue the good work and help others to achieve their potential too, and that way everyone can enjoy a happier and better life. We may even see some massive step changes in the way our companies and societies do business!

There are already a number of corporations and businesses implementing the principles of gratitude into their business models – I sincerely hope that we will see many more in years to come. Pioneers such as Chip Conolly at the Joie De Vivre Hotel chain are utterly sold on the culture changes they have seen since implementing a twice daily gratitude practice for all staff.

So, now you know why you aren't doing it, here are the five essential keys for transformation:

1. As the Nike commercial says "Just Do It!" Commit to your gratefulness practice – even if it is just writing down three things before you go to bed actually do it, and do it every day. Do not skip!!

2. Be genuine when you are saying thank you. You have got to mean it! Let it show in your smile and your eyes!

3. Remember that "What you appreciate, appreciates", so the more grateful you get, the more you will have to be grateful for.

4. Do it Together. By getting involved with others, family, colleagues or friends, you increase your potential for feeling happier – remember that when people actually called in the study I cited earlier, rather than just writing a few things down – they increased their happiness scores massively.

5. Finally, give thanks for what is to come – as if it is already real! Our brains are incredibly clever, but they have a few loopholes we can utilize and one of these is that the brain simply doesn't recognise the difference between reality and a vividly imagined illusion. So, if you can make it seem to your brain as if you already have the things you desire, and are already thankful for them, your brain will do its best to manifest them for you!

There are a number of ways to begin your gratefulness practice – I have chosen some of my favourites for you here. Some are from famous people, others are just simple common sense, but I hope that you will find one that will suit you as you begin this essential step towards a brighter and happier future.

1. ***Write Gratitude Letters***
You can write letters to the people in your life who have meant something to you, for whatever reason simply thanking them for their presence in your life, and the benefits that their advice or support have given you. I have even found it beneficial to write gratitude letters to people who I haven't had particularly great dealings with, because every one of them was sent into my life for a purpose so I could learn something new, and

that is empowering in its own way. By being grateful to them for the lesson learned, we can remove the negativity of being bullied, or made to feel unwanted.

2. ***Marianne Williamson (Facebook June 15th 2014):***
"At least once a day, stop long enough to allow yourself to be truly amazed by a tree, or a flower, or the sunlight dancing on land or sea. That is the sacred space, the place within us where we are witness to the ongoing miracles of life. And the more we are open to truly seeing them around us, the more we are able to truly feel them within us. Miracles are everywhere, all the time, waiting to be plucked by our awareness into the makings of a happy life."

3. ***Express your gratitude in person***
This one can be a little tough to start with, but start by making sure you thank staff in the local stores for their service, or the person on the end of the telephone when you have to call about your gas bill. Even if you have been unhappy with what the company has provided, these people are doing their best, and deserve our thanks for putting up with terrible wages and conditions to do a soul-destroying job where all they ever hear is complaints. Make their day – say thank you for their assistance in resolving the matter. Tell your best friend why you are so happy they are part of your life; tell your partner or spouse thank you even when they are doing something as mundane as the dishes! Trust me, once you start doing this you will find people itching to do even more for you because we all just love to be appreciated.

4. ***Prasanna Ranganathan*** – *Huffington Post Article July 17th 2014):*
Prasanna is legally blind, and though this has caused no end of struggles, it has taught him to value every day and to seize the moment wherever possible. I am currently trying to use his method in my daily practice. It is a rather beautiful one I think.

"I take what I call "mental gratitude pictures" and write about these pictures in my gratitude journal. Usually, this process involves me 1) pausing; 2) taking notice of a particular moment, image or detail around me; 3) taking a deep breath; 4) closing my eyes; and 5) envisioning the moment, image, or detail in my mind."

5. ***Express your gratitude in Art***
This is one for the <u>creative</u> amongst you, if you have artistic leanings of any kind – be it musical, literary, fine art, photography, pottery, etc. then you can make a small gift to say thank you to someone out of the blue.

You can also use this gift to maybe express your gratitude journal in a more visual way – cut out, draw or take pictures of the things you are grateful for and make a huge collage to put on your wall. Include whatever you are grateful for in your life, from your college sweetheart to cake!

6. *Tony Robbins – Unlimited Power Tape Series*

Tony likes to work out from himself in a spiral. I used this method when I first began my gratefulness practice and is one I recommend to my clients regularly. It is lovely and simple – simply start with yourself and work outwards in a spiral. He has a set order – and it is an order that I think is probably most apt – that it saves the least important things until last! You should start with yourself, both physical and mental things you are grateful for; then the people in your life and their physical and mental attributes that you most admire; then your pets etc; then your career and the things you own.

For example (you can get much more specific than this – but this gives you a rough outline):

'I am grateful for my heart, my knowledge and skills. I am grateful for my strong body and quick mind. I am grateful for my full hair and my excellent vision. I am grateful for my friends and their loving support of me whatever I do. I am grateful for my family, that they are strong and healthy. I am grateful for my pets, that they give me love so unconditionally. I am grateful for my career as a writer and the wonderful people who buy my books. I am grateful for my wonderful home and my wonderful possessions that make my life easier and brighter, etc.

7. *Make a Gratitude Date*

I love this idea that you make a date, set aside a specific time to sit down with your partner or your family to talk about all the things that you are all thankful for. We are supposed to do this on Thanksgiving, but how many of you just jump right into the Turkey and stuffing? It also shouldn't be just a once a year thing – make it daily, weekly, monthly, whatever works for your family, but do it and make it a part of your life as part of that bigger unit. Trust me, it really will improve the bonds between you and will even keep the cost at holidays and birthdays down a bit as people will chose items they really want not just what may give them the biggest status – as their self esteem will be so much higher their need to fit in with the crowd will lessen!

8. *Oprah Winfrey – Oprah's Life Class – YouTube*

Simply write three to five things down in your journal every day before you go to bed.

9. *Devote a specific time each day to gratitude*

This could be when you first get up, when you go to bed, just before meal times, or when you get in from work – whatever you choose stick to it. If you have a specific time it is far easier to make this stuff become a habit!

10. **_Use Social Media_**

This is a method I am using at the moment. I find it keeps me focussed and that I actually undertake my gratitude exercise each day. Having made a public commitment to doing so, I feel I have to do this for at least the month that I set out to do it to build it back into my life on a regular basis.

I post 3 things first thing in the morning, 3 at lunchtime, and then a further 3 just before I go to bed. I try to post at least one photograph a day, ideally one I have taken on my walk – to illustrate my thankfulness. It is a simple method, and I am finding it really is having an impact.

11. Try to pay attention to your day from a point of gratitude. Get amazed by all the goodness you usually take for granted. This fantastic YouTube video by TEDx Talks called "Gratitude" can get you in the right frame of mind for this.

12. If you are sitting in the office, a meeting, or even out with friends and you notice something or someone with a negative trait or attitude, try to switch it to a positive. An example might be a feeling of dread at spending all day in the conference room – try switching the thought by looking around you and finding something positive. Maybe the person leading the meeting is very positive and upbeat; maybe there is a great view from the window; maybe you are sitting next to your favourite colleague; even that your coffee is hot and tasty.

13. Gratitude requires humility, and it can be difficult to humble ourselves suitably to get the most from our gratitude practice. This fantastic article from Time is a great introduction to this under-appreciated virtue – it may help you to explore humility a little on yourself. http://healthland.time.com/2012/04/27/humility-a-quiet-underappreciated-strength/

14. Make sure you give at least one compliment to yourself a day, and one to someone else. This can be someone you love, or even a complete stranger. The compliment does not have to be something huge. It can be a simple "I really like your choice of top today, it really flatters you" to yourself as you look in the mirror; or "Thanks so much, that was lovely" to the waitress who collects your used coffee cup.

15. Try to look at things that go wrong as a learning opportunity. Rather than bemoaning the fact that everything always goes wrong, try to work out

what you can take forward from the experience, and be grateful for the lesson you will now not forget.

16. Try to take a day, just one day, where you do not moan or complain, criticize or gossip about others. This is a really tough call, but try and take note of how often you find yourself about to do this (don't beat yourself up if you slip occasionally, you are only human after all!) You will be amazed at how much energy and time you save by cutting out these non-productive and often negative actions and thoughts.

17. If someone calls you on the telephone, try to sound genuinely pleased that they have called. Too often it is easy to hear that the person on the other end is clearly harried and harassed and doesn't really want to talk to us. But a friend or loved one receiving this response one too many times will eventually stop calling all together. Sure we all have times when things are hectic – but it costs nothing to answer the phone with a bright and breezy "How lovely to hear your voice, I am so glad you called, but things are a little manic. Is it okay to ring back in a few minutes?"

18. Get involved with a cause that matters to you. Donate money, time or your skills. You will gain an even greater appreciation for the work that they do, and how great your life is in comparison with the people they are working with, that you will want to help even more. Charities are always incredibly appreciative of their donors and volunteers – they know they cannot function without them, so it is a great way to get some wonderfully positive feedback in your life for doing something you will find you need no gratitude to do because it means so much to you.

19. Mark anniversaries and birthdays with a new tradition. This is a wonderful practice, because it requires reflection on the past year in order to establish something you feel you wish to improve in your life or relationship. Write a letter full of excitement and hope about how your predictions for how the year ahead will pan out taking this new habit into consideration, and seal it tight. Then when you get to the next year go ahead and open it up to see how you got on!

20. Learn to appreciate a force bigger than yourself. People who have faith in God, the Universe, or any other greater force than themselves often see the world through the eyes of gratitude. So next time you see a beautiful flower, or feel a drop of rain or a snowflake settle on your face, lift you head and heart up to that higher power and say thank you to them for providing a world filled with beauty for you to enjoy. For more advanced knowledge on this, be sure to check out my enlightened book on Spirituality.

Chapter 5 – Want a little extra Happiness?

Though any of the above methods will be useful to you if you have just a little bit more time available in your day, you might want to consider adding in one of the following to truly boost your happiness potential – Mindfulness Practice; Meditation and Online Happiness Development Programs. These methods have been proven over and over again to massively improve mood; reduce symptoms of pain and depression; and even make people more productive and successful. Ask virtually any success coach, or any celebrity or sportsperson who has been at the top of their game for decades and they will extol the virtues of at least one of these! They will also express massive amounts of gratitude to the opportunities they have had in life; the people around them; and often a higher power for giving them such blessings too.

These three options do not replace our gratefulness practice though. They are add-ons that will increase the effectiveness and power of getting grateful for everything in your life – for a start they can help you get a better awareness of some of the things you have to be grateful for!

Meditation

Though meditation is not strictly a gratitude practice, it can become a very important part of your overall wellbeing and happiness practice. Meditation, like gratitude, has been scientifically proven to help with pain reduction; improved mood; better concentration; a healthier body; and to be able to lower levels of anxiety and depression, so whatever way you look at it you probably should try and make a little time in your day for it. I like to meditate using the things I have put down in my gratitude journal as affirmations, and I find that if I undertake my meditation practice after my gratitude practice at lunchtime I have a fantastically creative and productive afternoon.

It is so much simpler than most people believe to meditate, and don't think that you need to be able to sit still, and not think at all for hours on end – this would be biologically impossible for a start – our brains are always thinking, making sure our hearts pump and that we keep breathing! Start small. I started with the Wii game ZaZen – it just wanted you to sit and stare at a flickering candle for about three minutes. I got quite good at this – even when my cat thought it was a wonderful time to rub himself up against me and seek attention, I still stayed super still and focused on my candle! My continued success made me want to achieve longer times than the game would allow for, so I started to just light a candle, or look at a bunch of flowers and set a timer for about 5 minutes. I would just focus on it until the timer went off, and gradually, bit by bit I increased the time I set. I now happily zone out for a good twenty minutes most days. I sincerely believe that this ability to let go of my thoughts – without jumping into action to try and fix them, or dwell on them has made me more patient, and a much more relaxed person to be around!

The key thing to remember is that meditation is not the absence of thought, but it is all about how easy you find it to let your thoughts go without paying them any mind. So to start you will need a candle, and a timer. Light the candle and set the timer for just one minute. Focus only on the candle flame. Notice how it bends with the breeze, notice how the little wisps of smoke come off the top of the flame only. See how the flame is different colors in different areas. If other thoughts intrude, just let them go and refocus on the flame. Gradually increase the time you set as you get more comfortable sitting still and being peaceful.

You can choose to focus on your breath, or on a particular affirmation, or even get some guided meditation tapes. There are lots of great ones out there. Some are even based around gratitude – so enjoy exploring this wonderful and peaceful moment in your day. When you are done you will probably find it much easier to undertake your gratitude exercise – as you will be in tune with your inner self, and more open to the good in your life – rather than the negative stuff we normally cling to. My favorite audios to listen to come from Hypnosis Downloads.com ! I use them almost every day.

Mindfulness Practice

Mindfulness is often described as a meditation technique, but it is in so many ways much more than this. Mindfulness is a way of life. It takes some dedication to truly make it a part of your life, but once you have it embedded, you will find that your levels of satisfaction with life increases, physical and emotional pain becomes more easy to tackle and tolerate, and that you generally feel healthier and more grounded. Mindfulness is all about living in the now – being aware of yourself and your body as much as you can be.

Unlike meditation above in which the aim is to achieve a state of focused concentration on a sound, phrase, or thing (candle flame) to still the mind, mindfulness aims to achieve a non-judgmental acceptance of thoughts, feelings and sensations. Mark Williams of Oxford University's department of psychiatry calls it "direct knowing of what is going on inside and outside ourselves, moment by moment".

"It lets us stand back from our thoughts, and start to see their patterns," Williams said in an interview for the NHS. "Gradually we can train ourselves to notice when our thoughts are taking over, and realize that thoughts are simply 'mental events' that do not have to control us. Most of us have issues we find hard to let go of and mindfulness can help us deal with them more productively."

The method you need to follow to be able to use this method is this:

Simply start to gradually become more aware of your world. Take time to stop and notice the flowers in your neighbor's garden; pay attention to the smoothness of your cat's fur; really pay attention to the joy in your child's laugh; even notice exactly where your body may be in pain, and what kind of pain it is. You need to get out of cruise control, and really pay attention to what is actually happening in the moment. But don't judge, don't say that things are bad, or good – just take note of them, that they exist and that is okay.

Like our gratitude practice, or a standard meditation, it is a good idea to set a specific time for your mindfulness exercises. Though sitting in a quiet place, doing some deep breathing and tuning in sounds pretty straightforward, they do need you to be able to fully focus on them – so grabbing a minute before the school run, or snatching a minute or two in your lunch-break probably isn't ideal. Setting aside fifteen minutes a day to try and not let your mind wander, but keep it focused on your body, and training your mind to observe, focus and filter is pretty tricky – especially in the early days. You will be pleased to know that there are now plenty of centers who offer Mindfulness training, and you can even do an online search and find a lot of really good free courses to help you if you want to give it a try. I love to do it while on my daily walk. Also, HypnosisDownloads.com has a great "Mindfulness Meditation" download.

Online Happiness Courses

Finally, we come to online happiness courses. There are many of these out there, and price ranges go from free to $100's. I will be honest, unless you have a particular favorite happiness guru that is offering one, you can't go far wrong using the Berkely University's The Science of Greater Good's Online Course. It is free to use and lasts eight weeks. It is a truly great resource, and one I often recommend to clients. It covers all sorts of aspects of The Science of Happiness, including gratitude and is well worth the time you can spend on it. Plus, it has the added bonus of being based around all of their incredible research into this area – most of which has been truly outstanding and very useful in the writing of this book! You can also check out my incredible book on Happiness that goes very deep into the subject.

Chapter 6 – How to Make Gratitude a Habit

One of the things most people ask when they first start out to build a gratefulness habit is what on earth to be grateful for. Obviously, if you truly believe that you have nothing at all to be grateful for this could seem a really daunting task, and that making a habit out of being grateful is almost impossible. I tend to take a little time with people like this and start small. I ask them if there is a single part of their body, maybe that they like. I started with just a single freckle that I was quite fond of because I remembered my Dad telling me a daft story about it when it appeared when I was small.

Once we have them thinking about their cute button nose, or their long and elegant fingers, their fabulous handbag, or their wonderful best friend, I ask if there is a character trait that they think they might have that they admire. Many will look gloomy at this point, believing themselves to be beyond redemption – but I look at them and ask something like 'Do you think you are honest? I have felt that you have been very open with me about your concerns.' This gives them reassurance that I think that they are an honest person. I will often even ask them if they are really worried about what they think friends might say about them. These gentle questions are all to get people started. If they really cannot believe anything good about themselves, I try starting with things. If they drove to their appointment I might ask if they are grateful that they have a form of transport that got them here on time today. Did they notice the tulips in my neighbor's garden - are they grateful that they are so beautiful?

Note that I do not ask my clients if they are grateful for their car itself, or their body as a whole, or their personality as a whole. Many people are looking to trade up, or make changes in some way or another to pretty much everything in their lives, so if you ask about the object you will possibly end up with a litany of reasons why their car is so terrible, their body so ugly, and what a terrible person they are. I want you to try to look at what things do for you – rather than whether you like them. It is much easier to be proud of a body that can carry you where you need to go, than to try and say you love your body if you don't mean it. It is easier to be grateful for the convenience of being able to get where you want to go than it is for a car that has seen better days, and seems to need constant visits to the mechanic. Use cues from your environment – stop, take a deep breath and look around you. There will be something to be grateful for – even if it is just that there is a sidewalk or grass under your feet!

We all have something to be grateful for if we dig hard enough – be careful not to let yourself fall into the habit of saying "Nothing" or " I can't". These are absolute nightmares for your brain to try and work around because as soon as you say them they become true for your mind and are typical "depressive statements." Try to go with "I'll find something in a bit" or "I'll keep on looking" instead!

So, as a bit of a helper to get you started, here are some key questions to ask yourself :

1. What part of my body am I grateful for and why? (smooth skin; blue eyes; strong legs; dexterous fingers; curly hair; curvy shape; a single freckle, or anything else!)

2. Do I have any of the character traits I admire in others (honesty; courage; gratefulness; caring; adventurous; helpfulness; trustworthiness; hardworking, etc.)

3. What skills and knowledge do I have? (can you use a PC; read; write great essays; market things well; draw; paint; play an instrument; have specialist knowledge in some area.)

4. Do you have friends or family you are grateful to, and if you do why are you grateful that they are a part of your life? (Mom and Dad for supporting you through college; best friend for always being there with a bottle of wine and tub of ice cream when you are low; a nurse who helped you when you were sick; a tutor who passed on their passion for their subject; the postman for delivering your mail – anyone really!)

5. What things do you own? Do you have lots of things? If you own it and it is useful you should be grateful for it!

6. Finally, what things around you in your environment can you get grateful for? Do you enjoy hearing the birds sing in the morning? Does your neighbor or you have a beautiful garden? Are there any stunning buildings to look at on your way to work?

The key to gratitude is simply taking notice, of yourself and your own skills and abilities; of the people around you; the things around you; and your environment. Start taking notice, and getting grateful when you see something that makes you smile, or makes you think and you will find that the amount of things you have to be grateful for will increase.

However, I won't lie – getting disciplined enough to stick to your practice in the early days can be tough, because you are undertaking something new and that you have not yet built a habit for. So, the best time to undertake your gratitude practice is around one of those things that already is a habit for you! If you religiously clean your teeth at a specific time each day, try thinking about your things to be grateful for while you brush – then once finished go and write them down immediately.

I find that doing them literally as soon as I wake up before I even get out of bed, as I have my lunch and just as I am about to turn out the light before bed works best for me. My day can be a bit erratic between writing and therapy clients, so I find that these are the most regular times for me to fit my practice into to ensure I do it.

I have also found that doing your practice in the glare of public scrutiny also makes me much more likely to keep it up. Be sure to let people know your goal so that they can hold you accountable

So your keys for making this stick:

Daily Habits – This really doesn't take long to do, so it won't take long to get away from the thought that you just don't have the time. Because you will be feeling so much better you will also find that old worries and concerns simply do disappear, and so you will gain the time and energy you once wasted on them. So, just get on with it, and get grateful!

Weekly Habits – Try to make time for yourself on a weekly basis to enjoy a favorite or new hobby; relax in a sumptuous bubble bath; or just to sit peacefully in your garden. Check in with how you are feeling, and if there are any issues that need to be dealt with.

Monthly Habits – Schedule something special – a spa day or pamper session; a trip to a museum or gallery; a concert or play. Do something that lasts at least a few hours that you will really enjoy. It is important you get grateful and show yourself how important you are to yourself.

Lifetime Habits – Keep checking in, and don't ever get complacent. Do your practice daily and let it become as much a part of you as you hair, eyes or sense of humor! Deal with issues as they arise – don't put things off, and keep making sure you know just how special you are to yourself, and let those around you know just how special they are!

Conclusion

So, I hope you can now see just how vital getting grateful could be to improve the quality of your health; emotional wellbeing; relationships; career; social life; and overall happiness. It is such a simple technique to implement, but its effects are huge. There is literally no other practice out there that can deliver so much from so little effort.

I have shown you just how easy it is to foster an attitude of gratitude in your life, and you can choose to implement just one technique, build a small routine with two or three, or even go the whole hog and try and implement everything all at once – the choice is yours. However, I will give you my best advice as a personal advocate of many self help methods; and as a qualified therapist – go slow. Get one thing as a fully established habit before you add anything else into your daily practice.

We humans have a terrible tendency to be all or nothing types, and then we wonder why we 'fail' when we slip up at just one of the many things we try to implement all at once. Ever gone on a health kick, determined to lose weight, eat healthily, and exercise daily? How long did it last? I'm guessing not too long. Eventually we have to acknowledge the best way to do anything well is to ensure that we are focused entirely on that one thing until it has become a habit.

So, pick one method and stick with it until it is a natural to you as breathing. You may well find that by that time that you have already seen a massive increase in your gratitude and you are unknowingly doing some of the other suggestions in this book anyway – but keep it simple so you don't fail. You just need a few minutes a day, and you will see all the benefits I have discussed in this book.

I hope this book was able to help you to understand how powerful gratitude is, and just how easy it is to start a gratitude practice.

The next step is to get cracking, and get grateful!

Finally, if you discovered at least one thing that has helped you or that you think would be beneficial to someone else, be sure to take a few seconds to easily post a quick positive review. As an author, your positive feedback is desperately needed. Your highly valuable five star reviews are like a river of golden joy flowing through a sunny forest of mighty trees and beautiful flowers! *To do your good deed in making the world a better place by helping others with your valuable insight, just leave a nice review.*

My Other Books and Audio Books
www.AcesEbooks.com

Peak Performance Books

Health Books

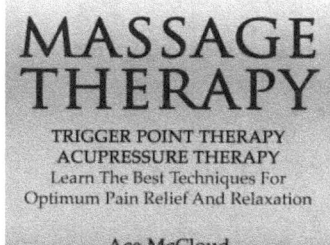

Be sure to check out my audio books as well!

 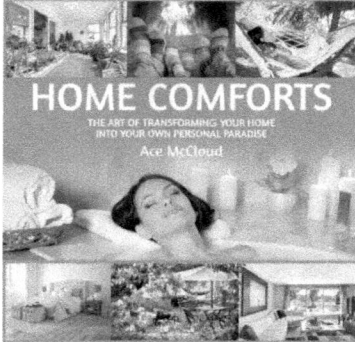 

  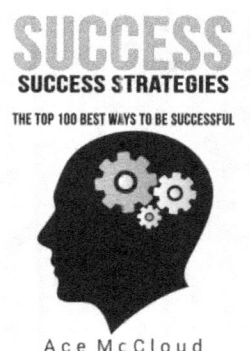

Check out my website at: **www.AcesEbooks.com** for a complete list of all of my books and high quality audio books. I enjoy bringing you the best knowledge in the world and wish you the best in using this information to make your journey through life better and more enjoyable! **Best of luck to you!**

www.ingramcontent.com/pod-product-compliance
Lightning Source LLC
Chambersburg PA
CBHW051427070526
44584CB00023B/3615